Teacher's Selection:
Anthology of Fifth Grade Poetry

1998 Edition
Volume XX

Published by Anthology of Poetry, Inc.

Teacher's Selection:
Anthology of Fifth Grade Poetry©
1998 Edition
Volume XX

Printed in the United States of America

Authors responsible for originality
of poems submitted.

The Anthology of Poetry, Inc.
P.O. Box 698 • 307 East Salisbury
Asheboro, NC   27204-0698

ISBN: 1-883931-14-2

Our belief that children live and think in poetic images is again confirmed by the poetry of this edition. If you want to know what is on the minds of our children, poetry is the window. This edition will let you look through that window to a world prose could never describe. To a world painted with wonder, awe and sometimes confusion, with microscopic inspection of subjects that adults hardly notice and with insight into issues adults also struggle with.

The Anthology of Poetry proudly presents to you the hard bound edition of *Teacher's Selection: Anthology of Fifth Grade Poetry*. The poems of this edition are the top honors from fifth grade classrooms from across the United States. Of all entries from each school only a few receive nominations for publication by each fifth grade teacher. And of those nominations only three are selected for publication. Congratulations.

We thank the fifth grade teachers for their participation in this project and, as always, we applaud the poets who shared their gifts.

We look forward to the publication of upcoming editions of *Teacher's Selection: Anthology of Fifth Grade Poetry*.

The Editors

Pain

I'm talking pain!
I'm talking cramps!
I'm talking hurt, burn, suffer!
I'm talking bite, prick, sting, injure!
I'm talking strain, stress, torment, sprain, heartburn!
I'm talking ache, twitch, tingle, agony, arthritis, spasm!
I'm talking pang, sore, break, grieve, distress, irk, throb!
I'm talking PAIN!

Jimmy Spickler

Helen Muraski Elementary
Strongsville, OH
Nominated by fifth grade teacher Mary E. Holman

Quiet

I'm talking about quiet.
I'm talking about a baby's breath quiet.
I'm talking about quiet.
I'm talking about a mother's secret touch quiet.
I'm talking about quiet.
I'm talking about a cool breeze on
an early spring morning quiet.
I'm talking about quiet.
I'm talking about a little mouse's footsteps
as he scurries through a house quiet.
I'm talking about quiet.
I'm talking about Martin Luther King, Jr.
when he thought about peace quiet.
I'm talking about quiet.
I'm talking about walking through a forest
when nothing is moving quiet.
I'm talking about quiet.
I'm talking about butterflies when
they flutter their wings quiet.
I'm talking about quiet.

Robert M. Waltzer

Helen Muraski Elementary
Strongsville, OH
Nominated by fifth grade teacher Mary E. Holman

Short

I'm talking short!
I'm talking small!
I'm talking skimpy, stumpy, tiny!
I'm talking dwarfed, compact, stocky, little!
I'm talking close to the ground, stunted, stubby,
low, sawed-off!
I'm talking dumpy, chunky, runty, undersized,
abbreviated, not tall!
I'm talking diminutive, slight, condensed, abrupt,
squat, concise, terse!
I'm talking SHORT!

Cody Lee Ginter

Helen Muraski Elementary
Strongsville, OH
Nominated by fifth grade teacher Mary E. Holman

The Wind

The wind is very soft, the wind floats in the air.
The gentle wind flying by like a horse.
Flying as fast as it can.

But, Wait!!
The wind suddenly stopped!! Where did the wind go?
I can't feel its soft feeling!!
It must come back soon!
I hope it comes back soon.

Wait!!! I feel something. Something like a soft feather!
It's the wind! It's the wind!
I'm glad the winds are back.

Jason Morvan

St. Piusx
Bedford, OH
Nominated by fifth grade teacher Sr. Kathleen

Seasons!

Spring is here with sun and flowers.
Rain showers come and go.
Summer follows with hot, hot sun.
Lots of things to do.
Bike rides, swimming, flying kites.
Fall is here with lots of colors.
Cool winds start to blow.
Winter blows in with white icy snow.
Christmas lights and shiny stars.
All the seasons are fun!

Allyson Sierputowski

St. Piusx
Bedford, OH
Nominated by fifth grade teacher Sr. Kathleen

Boots My Pet Rabbit

I have a great pet -- her name is Boots.
She is the best pet ever!

She brings love and pleasure to me
when my days are so dreary,
she likes to run and scoot
when her days are bright and cheery.

My pet is a rabbit with one bad habit.
She likes to sleep during the day
and stay up at night to cause havoc!

Boots likes to drink a lot of water,
she reminds me of a little otter.
But what can I say --
because she is here to stay
and I wouldn't want to be without her.

Nicole Kozak

St. Piusx
Bedford, OH
Nominated by fifth grade teacher Sr. Kathleen

I pretend nothing has changed,
but I know I'm wrong.
I pretend to see sunshine,
to chase my sorrow away.
I pretend to be strong,
so that others may.
I pretend nothing has changed
in my life today.

Joy Weigand

Santrock Elementary School
Barberton, OH
Nominated by fifth grade teacher William J. Marshall

My First Day On The School Bus

My first day on the school bus
Was scarier than ever before.
It pulled up in my driveway,
As the driver opened the door,
It hit me in my face.
While I was unconscious,
I dreamt of outer space.
When I was awakened from my misery,
I knew that that was the last day on the school bus.
At least for me!
But my mother made me step on.
I wasn't comfortable with this,
Friends said, "Come on, come on,"
So I braved it as I stepped on.
Then I hurried to step on,
But then I was saddened
'Cause my mother was nowhere to be found.
I fell and almost fainted and soon began to cry.
Why would my mother leave me?
Why? Why? Why?

I arrived at school,
But uh-oh, a li'l nauseated I felt.
Unfastening my belt, walking with knees knocking,
I sure hoped tomorrow the bus wouldn't be rocking.
Or this school bus ride would be my first
And last ride!

Tristan Lawrence

Glover Elementary
Akron, OH
Nominated by fifth grade teacher T. Noland

If I Was...

If I was a butterfly
I would fly
Through the sky
To the tops of trees so very high.

If I was a dog
I would be thankful I wasn't a frog.
I would roam through the fog
And on the farm chase the hog.

If I was a bat
I wouldn't be fat
'Cause I would spend time
Flying away from the hungry cat.
And sleep upside down...what do ya' think of that?

That's all if I was an animal,
But I'm just a human -- yet still a mammal.
So in a way,
We're all the same day-by-day.

Courtney Lee RoseKelly

Glover Elementary
Akron, OH
Nominated by fifth grade teacher T. Noland

The Tower

The gigantic tower creeps up high
Into a cloudless evening sky
Even in the strongest wind it stands idle
Like a star during its nighttime recital.
It reflects the sun with its abundance of glass
Like an urban mirror with enormous mass.
And at dusk when it shows its light,
All is still in the bright open night.
In the city it stands like a looming giant
Over a building called Wriggs and Bryant.
Everyone watches with fascination,
As they shoot fireworks from it on a special occasion.
You can see its top only when the skies are clear
As this tower's peak is far not near.
It's three hundred fifty meters to the summit
Where nobody can take anything from it.
People admire its beauty everyday
As in its shadow children laugh and play.
When people look at it glowing so bright
It sends a heartwarming beacon that says good night.

Nicholas Foore

Manchester Middle School
Akron, OH
Nominated by fifth grade teacher Nancy Grimes

My Life is All in a Ball

I remember my first year in basketball,
I have to admit I couldn't ball at all.
When coach needed a dependable player
to shoot the three,
He wouldn't even bother to look at me.

My crossover was weak, my jumper was broke,
And everyone went in shock when I hit a stroke.
The basketball was bigger than me...
I was the size of a tick.
When we played sandlot basketball
I was last to be picked.

Though I tried to the best of my ability,
no one was ever pleased.
Every time I came to practice I was being teased.
I was the smallest player on the team
and I was pretty small.
The rest of the players on the team
were pretty much tall.

On defense, it was normal for me
to get taken to the rack.
A five-year-old could cross me
with one hand behind his back.

My status of even making a lay-up
was just "possibly."
I couldn't even drive
without fearing someone swatting me.

I had no "ups" and definitely couldn't rebound
Whenever I even tried...I jumped up and fell down.
When our team had a three-point shooting contest
I got disqualified.
I jumped over the line every time I tried.

I air-balled foul shots throughout the season.
As you can see, I was sorry for many reasons.
I lost my temper and got ejected...
the refs weren't going to allow it.
I said, "But the team needs me"
...other players said "I doubt it."

It broke my heart when I didn't get a trophy
at the end of the year.
I congratulated other players
while fighting back tears.
I needed more than practice -- I needed skills.
I had to hope and pray that on the first day back
I'd show coach I was for real.

At the end of that season I got two trophies
For best sportsmanship and M.V.P.
Now I have five coaches wanting to recruit me.
At eighteen, in college playing ball
is where I hope to be.

Ricco Beard

Glover Elementary
Akron, OH
Nominated by fifth grade teacher T. Noland

The Traveler

I've longed to see the U.S.A.,
I'll get to fulfill my dream today.
New York, Chicago and Idaho,
Jump in my car and off I go.
Roads and highways everywhere,
They can take me anywhere.
I check my map to guide my way,
I sure don't want to get lost today.
Down the highway, I check my speed,
A speeding ticket I don't need.
Thinking of postcards I will send,
Took a left at the light, oops dead end!!!

Colby Cox

Roosevelt Elementary
McDonald, OH
Nominated by fifth grade teacher Connie Morris

A Baseball Player's Life

When your dad gives you your first
baseball and bat,
Then you get your favorite team hat.
He shows you how to hit,
Then you get a baseball mitt.

You play catch all day,
Then in the month of May,
You sign up for Little League
But it's really hard to succeed.

Your dad keeps pushing you,
And you just want to get through.
Finally, you get to play.
You play and hey.....

You're pretty good.
And all along your dad knew you could.
You finish up with Little League
And you did succeed.

You go to high school and play your heart out
And never shout and pout.
You think you're good enough for the show
But your dad says "No."

Go to college, work on your skills,
Do better at hitting, run some hills.
While at college, play really hard ball,
Then you've almost done it all.

After college ball, you get the call.
You zoom past Rookie league, A ball,
Double AA in a flash,
And you earn a little cash.

You're stuck in Triple AAA ball
Waiting for a call.
Then it's finally time
And you sing like a chime.

You're going to the Majors you say,
All right!!! Yeah!!!
You stay in the Majors about ten years
And you have your share of fears and tears.
Then you think your baseball days are going to crash
But you're still earning a little cash.

You start to fear
It may be your last year,
Your teammates are having fun.
You can't believe you're almost done.

Then you get the call
And......
You know you're done with baseball.

Michael Nettling

Pfeiffer
Akron, OH
Nominated by fifth grade teacher Annmarie Crofoot

Stars

At night the stars
Seem very near.
But they are
So far from here.

The stars at night
Are so bright.
And are such
A magnificent sight.

I wish I could live
On a star.
Although they are
So very far.

At night I dream
The stars are near.
So I could live
Not far from here.

At night the stars
Seem very near.
But they are
So far from here.

Ashley Lynn Stitt

Roosevelt Elementary
McDonald, OH
Nominated by fifth grade teacher Connie Morris

The snow is lovely.
The thunder is horrible.
The rain is okay.

Joshua Maus

Roosevelt Elementary
Warren, OH
Nominated by fifth grade teacher Frank Barile

Sky Hawk

A hawk is prowling.
Its claws are in the blue air;
Does it really care?

Dominique DeSanti

Roosevelt Elementary
Warren, OH
Nominated by fifth grade teacher Bobbie Patterson

The Sea

T he sea is teeming with life.
H aving waves billow over you.
E verlasting is the water of the sea.

S urfing over the tumbling waves.
E nter the great world of the sea.
A man on the shore gawking at the sea's greatness.

Julian Muller

Akiva Academy
Youngstown, OH
Nominated by fifth grade teacher Barbara K. Oddis

Heaven

Beyond the clouds there is a place
where there can be no harm.
Beyond the clouds there is a place
where nothing will ever go wrong.
Beyond the clouds there is a place
where people go to rest.
Beyond the clouds there is a place
where the ground is made of beautiful charms.

Beyond the clouds there is a place
where everybody would like to be.
Beyond the clouds there is a place
where angels get their wings.
Beyond the clouds there is a place
where you can see the world.
Beyond the clouds there is a place,
this place is right for me.

Irene Stevens

St. Matthias
Youngstown, OH
Nominated by fifth grade teacher Maria Batcha

Collecting

I collect things
this and that,
especially baseball cards and big fat cats.
I collect things
especially rubber bands,
and lots of farmland.
I collect things all the time,
I collect everything, even dimes.

Andy Pokrivnak

St. Matthias
Youngstown, OH
Nominated by fifth grade teacher Maria Batcha

The Olympics

I watched the Olympics all the time,
The skiers had their chance to shine.
The world awaited the results,
Tara skated without fault.
They jumped they even seemed to fly,
They twirled until they reached the sky.
The skiers were an amazing sight,
They actually seemed to take flight.
And don't forget those great big jumps,
And all those other little bumps.

Betsy Bruchs

St. Edward School
Youngstown, OH
Nominated by fifth grade teacher Kathy Kelly

Spring

Pretty flowers grow in spring
They have new life and that's a joyful thing

The sun shines and shows its face
I'll ride my bike in that sunny space

Spring is a time for new growth
The trees and the flowers love this both

One day I looked down
And saw a caterpillar frown

I asked it why it was so sad
He answered, "Why? I am glad!"

We had become such best friends
We'd never wanted the day to end

I noticed the spring air smelling so sweet
What I'm saying is that spring is neat

Evelyn Akpadock

St. Edward School
Youngstown, OH
Nominated by fifth grade teacher Kathy Kelly

Presidents

Presidents are our nation's leaders.
They can have a beard, a moustache, both, or neither.
Some are dirty;
Some are clean.
Some are nice;
Some are mean.
Some are fat;
Some are thin.
Some are an only child;
Some are a twin.
Some wear glasses;
Some wear a hat.
Some have a dog;
Some have a cat.
Presidents say what goes, just like kings.
They can be most anything.

Anthony Yurcho

St. Brendan School
Youngstown, OH
Nominated by fifth grade teacher Mary Connell

My Dream

I once had a dream, it wasn't that scary
I met a weird guy and he called himself Larry
He was green, no brown (well, I don't know)
But he was neatly tied in a tight little bow.

So I untied him as fast as I could
And pried him out with a purple stick of wood
He was stuck in a suitcase all tied up like that
With only his tiny little hat.

Then he took off his hat and said, "Well hello!"
And led me to a big bowl of Jell-O
He said, "This is my home, do you like the design?"
I said, "Your house's design looks mighty fine."

A herd of monsters was running straight ahead
For a minute there, I thought I was dead!
(Until I fell out of bed.)

Bridgette Celio

St. Brendan School
Youngstown, OH
Nominated by fifth grade teacher Mary Connell

Basketball

B eing in the action
A t the gym
S uper fun
K ind of tiring
E arly in the morning
T otally fun
B eing part of the team
A ll of the fun
L eaving the court
L onging to play ball

Ben-Ami Kessler

Akiva Academy
Youngstown, OH
Nominated by fifth grade teacher Barbara K. Oddis

Embarrassment

Embarrassment is tripping over your own two feet,
Wetting your bed, and a bright spotlight.
EMBARRASSMENT is the taste of spinach.
Unwanted rice and molding cabbage
Smell embarrassing.

Boys make me feel embarrassed.
EMBARRASSMENT is the sound of laughing
And crying.
EMBARRASSMENT is in the locker room,
In the streets, and in the schools.

EMBARRASSMENT is horrifying!
Embarrassment is bright red.
Embarrassment is me.

Antonette Joseph

St. Brendan School
Youngstown, OH
Nominated by fifth grade teacher Mary Connell

Father Time

Every year we age as time goes by.
Father Time takes old lives,
Yet he gives back the lives he takes.
He has outlived us all.

Life could not go on without Father Time because,
Without time we wouldn't have a past or a future.
Through time he teaches us new ways.
Through him we have gotten our technology.
Without Father Time we would live
In a pointless world.

Father Time gives us sadness or happiness.
He guides us with our lives.
He tries to bring joy everywhere.
We get our loved ones because of him.

Time passes by slowly or quickly.
Father Time gives us bad times,
But makes up for it with good times.
If Father Time could go back would he change that?

Sarah Ann Sledd

Frank Ohl Middle School
Austintown, OH
Nominated by fifth grade teacher Barbara Adair

Red

Red is the color of many things,
Our chairs at school and robin's red wings,
The red headband that I wear on my head,
A thermometer; these things are all red.
The nice, cozy slippers that I wear on my feet.
My face when I'm embarrassed, it looks like a beet.
The beautiful red that's in a rainbow,
The sunset when the sun's sinking so low.
Red is the color that makes me feel mad.
But some other times it makes me feel sad.
Red is the color of blood when I lose a tooth.
It's also the color of the First Aid Booth.
Red, red, red, red...
All these things are red.

Tekla Toman

St. Christine School
Youngstown, OH
Nominated by fifth grade teacher Kelli Leonard

Hellos

Hi, hello, how do you do?
Hola, allo, wie geht's? Ciao
A wave, a nod, a handshake too,
A hug, or a kiss from your great-aunt Sue.
These are all ways to say hello
In every single way I know.
Now you know twelve different ways
To say hello twelve different days.
So I hope that you will say hello
To everybody that you know.

Lindsay Miller

St. Christine School
Youngstown, OH
Nominated by fifth grade teacher Kelli Leonard

Orange

Orange is a fast tiger hiding behind a tree.
Orange is a sweet-smelling mum on a fall day.
Orange is a smooth clay pot where flowers are grown.
Orange is a fuzzy peach waiting to be eaten.
Orange is a shiny pumpkin so nicely round.
Orange is a tasty candy corn sitting in a bowl.
Orange is a delicious pumpkin pie cut in slices.
Orange is an old rusted nail that cannot be used.
Orange is a sweet tangerine freshly peeled.
Orange is a gorgeous sunset
  Setting behind the mountain.

Lauren Loncar

St. Christine School
Youngstown, OH
Nominated by fifth grade teacher Kelli Leonard

Why?

Why is the world the way it is?
Why does one think that it is all his?
Why can't everyone just share?
Or soon the world will be caught in a tear.
Where do I go?
I think I'm smart enough to know.
Why do people do drugs?
Soon they won't be able to give hugs.
Why do people kill others?
Why do people take kids from their mothers?
But all the questions I will ask
I'll just take off my mask and ask
Why is the world the
Way it is?

Brian Mellott

Frank Ohl Middle School
Austintown, OH
Nominated by fifth grade teacher Barbara Adair

Rainy Days

Rainy weather is a bore
There always seems to be more
And more
Maybe if I were a raindrop
It wouldn't be so boring
But since I'm me
I'm sitting here snoring

Collin Emerick

Louisville Elementary
Louisville, OH
Nominated by fifth grade teacher Judy Surmay

I Know A Girl Who Used To Drink

I know a girl who used to drink,
She had trouble, she didn't think.
I told her not to drink like Uncle Mac,
But when I did she turned her back.

Later on she joined a gang,
Someone shot her with a bang.
Luckily she was fine,
Until she took a drink of wine.

Then again she started to smoke,
And got interested in a drug called coke.
I think she took life as a joke,
In third grade she promised me she wouldn't smoke.

She did all sorts and kinds of drugs,
And hung out with a lot of thugs.
I hope you never do that stuff,
Then your life will get real tough.

But now she lays beneath the ground,
No trace of her to be found.
What a waste of life and soul,
Just to fertilize the earth below.

Meghan McCaulley

Louisville Elementary
Louisville, OH
Nominated by fifth grade teacher Judy Surmay

Fishing

Out on the bank
Of a crooked creek.
I sit and wait
For a tug on my bait.

A sudden pull on your line!
A tenseness of your spine.
Reel! Reel! Pull! Pull!
Now your stomach will be full.

David Benninger

Wooster Christian School
Wooster, OH
Nominated by fifth grade teacher Tammy Starkey

Doggie Heaven

Do doggies go to Heaven?
If they don't, where do they go?
I have had a lot of dogs
And they all die I know

Do dogs go to Heaven?
My mommy says they do
So when you go to Heaven
You'll see them again too

One, two, three, four
Is there a Heaven for dogs galore?
Five, six, seven, eight
They go marching through the gate

Is there a doggie Heaven
I wonder if it's true
If there's a doggie Heaven
Some people would turn blue

Some people don't believe it
They say it's mighty fine
But I know what they're thinking
They'd rather drink turpentine

Is there a doggie Heaven?
I often ask my dad
I ask it over and over
I think he's going mad

I now know the answer
I don't ask anymore
There is a doggie Heaven
It's filled with dogs galore

One, two, three, four
There is a Heaven for dogs galore
Five, six, seven, eight
They go marching through the gate
Of doggie Heaven

Kate Sheehan

Marshallville Elementary
Marshallville, OH
Nominated by fifth grade teacher Thomas Cleary

Winter

Winds blowing snow around,
Drifting high upon the ground,
You can tell Mr. Frost has been here,
He always comes 'round this time of year.

Children go run and play,
For it's their favorite time of day.
They build their forts strong and high,
Then they let their snowballs fly.

Scott Amstutz

Wooster Christian School
Wooster, OH
Nominated by fifth grade teacher Tammy Starkey

Martin Luther King

M anly
A rmed with the Bible
R esponsive to the times
T enderhearted
I ntuitive
N ot blaspheming

L eading
U nderstanding
T ruthful
H elpful
E nthusiastic
R eactive

K ind
I rritated about separation
N ational figure
G entle

Douglas R. Anderson

Wooster Christian School
Wooster, OH
Nominated by fifth grade teacher Tammy Starkey

Challenger

Challenger went into a skyward motion,
Didn't know about the coming explosion,
It was so amazing,
Its engines were blazing,
But then it soon fell to the ocean.

Remember seven astronauts we hold so dear,
They were so brave -- they had no fear,
We give to them a grand salute,
And with our hearts a bold tribute,
Although their bodies have left the earth --
Their spirits will always be here.

Devin A. Draudt

Melrose Elementary
Wooster, OH
Nominated by fifth grade teacher Patricia Chelf

Sled Riding

I like sled riding in the winter.
I also like the sound of the snow crunching under me.
Crunch!
Crunch!
CRUNCH!
Under my green, circular sled.

Andy Blind

Canton Christian Academy
Canton, OH
Nominated by fifth grade teacher Gretchen Shaffer

Colors Of The Rainbow

People are like the colors of the rainbow.
They come in many different shapes and sizes.
No one person should be a part of anyone's
prizes or surprises.
They can be African-American, American,
Native American, Chinese, Japanese, Hispanic,
Jewish or Russian.
We all are in this world together,
and together forever.

Oheneba Kofi Amponsah

Madge Youtz Elementary
Canton, OH
Nominated by fifth grade teacher Theresa M. Barbato

Stars

MERCURY, VENUS, EARTH and MARS
are just the names of a few of the stars,
JUPITER, SATURN,
AND ALPHA CENTAURI,
boy at night it still gets starry!
If I had one wish,
I guess it would be,
that the stars are always there,
for someone else to see!!

Bryan Grantz

Madge Youtz Elementary
Canton, OH
Nominated by fifth grade teacher Theresa Barbato

One Of Those Days

JUST ONE OF THOSE DAYS

I woke up this morning,
And fell out of bed,
Then when I felt the bump on my head,
I said,
It's one of those days.

I went to the bathroom,
Squirted toothpaste everywhere,
Then when I felt it in my hair,
I said,
It's one of those days.

I came home from school,
Dropped my books on my foot,
When I felt the welt on my foot,
I said,
It's one of those days.

I went to my room,
And tripped over the broom,
When I felt the splinter in my foot,
I said,
It's one of those days.

Hallelujah the day's over,
Now I'm going to bed,
And I hope when I wake up,
I don't fall on my head!

Kaitlin Bristow

Walker Elementary School
Canton, OH
Nominated by fifth grade teacher Marge Oliver

Spring

Springtime is getting near.
It is my favorite time of year.
Sounds of birds fill the air.
Signs of spring are everywhere.
Flowers are blooming,
Trees are budding,
And the grass is turning green.
It is the prettiest sight I have ever seen!
Spring is getting near I can hardly wait.
Please spring don't be late!

Brittany Brinkman

Walker Elementary School
Canton, OH
Nominated by fifth grade teacher Marge Oliver

Kindness

Kindness is hot pink.
It makes me feel like I have saved a life.
Like a police officer who has just jumped
In front of a bullet.
I feel kindness
When I teach someone how to do something.
Kindness is lovely.

Rebekah Welden

Canton Christian Academy
Canton, OH
Nominated by fifth grade teacher Gretchen Shaffer

Wintertime

The fluffy white snow,
Drifting down to the earth,
Looking like little shreds of soap,
Just cut,
Landing on houses,
trees,
and people!

Michelle Wright

Canton Christian Academy
Canton, OH
Nominated by fifth grade teacher Gretchen Shaffer

Friendships

Friendships are things
That can't be broke,
Even over a
Simple joke.

Friendships will last
Forever and ever,
No matter how, when,
Why or whatever.

Friendships are meant
To be kept,
You should always
Intercept.

Karestyn Robinson

Walker Elementary School
Canton, OH
Nominated by fifth grade teacher Marge Oliver

The Bed

I don't want to get out of bed,
But my mom said
I would hurt my head
If I don't get out of bed.
I told her I like my head,
But I don't want to get out of bed.
The next day I said
I will get out of bed
And use my head!

Elizabeth Smith

St. Edward
Ashland, OH
Nominated by fifth grade teacher Laurie Keller

Daffodils

Daffodils are flowers
That you can look at for hours.
They come in the spring
When the birds start to sing.
You see them on cards
Or in people's yards.
They come in orange, yellow, and white.
If you want to see one, you just might!

Jennifer Ditlevson

St. Edward
Ashland, OH
Nominated by fifth grade teacher Laurie Keller

Coffee

When my dad wakes
up early Sunday morning,
he goes
downstairs
and makes his

s
t
e
a
m
i
n
g

hot coffee. Then
the smell travels
upstairs and awakes us all.
We go
downstairs
and watch
him slowly, quietly, lift the glass up
and
then
put

it
back
down.
Later at night as he
is tucking me in bed I
can smell the coffee on his mustache.

Lee A. Downing

Riley Elementary
Fostoria, OH
Nominated by fifth grade teacher Melissa Depinet

Dad

My dad always has a funny smell.
A smell I can only smell.
Right after work the aroma of
his carpentry job fills the air.
A picture forms,
a picture forms of his job, and him.
And then again I smell that smell
of wood, and dust, and smoke.

Elizabeth A. Lombardy

Riley Elementary
Fostoria, OH
Nominated by fifth grade teacher Melissa Depinet

Mr. Hunter

As Mr. Hunter blows his whistle
upon the wrestling deck,
I hear it and am annoyed,
as I stop and pay attention.
My wrestling coach, loud, rude, tall,
Mr. Hunter, whom I love above all.

William D. Reese III

Riley Elementary
Fostoria, OH
Nominated by fifth grade teacher Melissa Depinet

Hummingbird

H ummingbird beautiful hummingbird.
U are
M y beautiful hummingbird.
M y beautiful
I ntelligent hummingbird is
N othing short of
G raceful.
B ecause,
I n my heart you'-
R e my
D arling hummingbird.

Jared Hoffman

McCormick Middle School
Huron, OH
Nominated by fifth grade teacher Patrick Norwell

Everything

I see with my imagination, brilliant colors,
as if a rainbow covers my mind.

A bat flies through the night sky
threatening to eclipse the full moon.

A tree blocking the simple rays
of the giant burning ball of gasses.

The school stands, standing in front of a field,
but not any field.
The field of life, usually football is played on it
yet so many other things go on during school,
but no one cares.

I see with my imagination, everything and anything,
anything and everything possible,
but the impossible still stands in this barrier.

Clay Pilkenton

McCormick Middle School
Huron, OH
Nominated by fifth grade teacher Patrick Norwell

Untold Questions?

When you wake up every morning
do you think of life, how things work or the universe.
I ask you is life a blur or just another dimension?
I ask again are we just ants
or mortals with a consequence?
Can you see beyond the black holes over the universe
or are you told how far to look.
Maybe you are only another human.
Because there are thousands of others.
Why are we here it's a question you hear
almost everywhere you go.
I speak too much you might say
but maybe I see untruthful sense,
but I think the only reason you say this is
it's a large place where dogs eat cats.
And human class can't seem to live with that.

Matthew Jacobs

McCormick Middle School
Huron, OH
Nominated by fifth grade teacher Patrick Norwell

Black

Black is a silent room.
It is a bug waiting to meet its doom.
Black is a velvet sky.
It is the question "Why?"
Black is the darkness of midnight.
It is the dress that fits just right.
Black is the shadow that follows you.
It is the little number two.
Black is a ballpoint pen.
It is what happened then.
Black is a pair of sunglasses.
It is a dog that passes by.
Black is the color of a paintbrush.
It is the sound of a hush.
Black is the deep, deep sea.
It is the color which describes me.

Aubrey Meade

St. Peter School
Huron, OH
Nominated by fifth grade teacher Ms. Fry

About Bugs Bunny

Bugs Bunny,
Is so funny.
He doesn't hop like a bunny.
He eats a carrot,
Like a parrot,
But he doesn't like to share it.

Meredith Leigh Skaggs

St. Peter School
Huron, OH
Nominated by fifth grade teacher Ms. Fry

Life is Like a Symphony

Life is like a symphony,
It has its high notes and its low notes.
They can be short or long.
Proclaim a song or condemn a soul,
But you must remember
This symphony will always end,
Whether on a low note or on a high note
It is your choice.

Alyssa Murray

St. Peter School
Huron, OH
Nominated by fifth grade teacher Ms. Fry

The Dancing Stars

Once I scooped up some
dancing stars from the river
in a water pail.

Tyler D. Sampson

Melmore Elementary
Melmore, OH
Nominated by fifth grade teacher Sharon Chamberlain

The Tiger

The tiger strong and fierce,
moves out of his den
to find something to eat.

So he moves through the grass
so smooth and fine and
sees a prey ahead.

So he ducks down low
then runs through the grass
like the flowing waters.
Then carries it home in his mouth.

Jaimie R. Amory

Melmore Elementary
Melmore, OH
Nominated by fifth grade teacher Sharon Chamberlain

Earth

Round, beautiful
twirling, swirling, whirling
smooth, soft, lovely, wonderful
Circle

Ashley Williams

Auburn Elementary School
Shelby, OH
Nominated by fifth grade teacher Doug Plice

Friendship

If you are a friendly person
you will grow up to find
that people don't always like the ones
that are always kind.
You can choose what you want
and you choose what you please;
you can even choose your best friend
as long as they're not a tease.

Carli Cushing

Stadium Elementary School
Mansfield, OH
Nominated by fifth grade teacher Barry Woodhull

America

America, America
America's my homeland,
America's my pride.
America still lives,
America will never die 'cause,
in my heart she will survive.
America! America!

Summer Hicks

Stadium Elementary School
Mansfield, OH
Nominated by fifth grade teacher Barry Woodhull

What I Love

I love hugs
and
I love kisses
but
what I love
most is help
with the
dishes.

Washing and scrubbing
that's not what I do.
So please HELP HELP
me

Oh please.

I will get it done just wait
and see.

Gera Sorrell

Wildwood Elementary School
Middletown, OH
Nominated by fifth grade teacher Dana Miller

Swimming

Backstroke, butterfly
All the strokes are fun.
Breaststroke, freestyle
Work hard to be number one.
The times are getting faster,
Time to set another goal.
Practicing hard for the big meet,
Starts, kick, and pull.
The big meet comes,
I'm on the block,
Can I do it?
I will not stop.
The gun goes off
Goggles in place.
Eat my bubbles
This is my race!

Kristin Leigh Raab

Waynesville Elementary
Waynesville, OH
Nominated by fifth grade teacher Mrs. Campbell

Love

Love is stupid
Love is dumb
Love is like old bubble gum
I'll never love anyone
But that kid that sits
Two rows behind me
Is kind of cute.

Sandy Bouman

Waynesville Elementary
Waynesville, OH
Nominated by fifth grade teacher Mrs. Denier

The Football Season

The fall is here it's time to begin,
I really wish our team could win.
The football, the helmets, pads and gear,
we love to hear the crowd cheer.
It takes a lot of practice and sweat,
we're just not the best quite yet.
November's here it's time to end,
we'll come back next year and try again.

Josh Richardson

Waynesville Elementary
Waynesville, OH
Nominated by fifth grade teacher Mrs. Bell

You Were There For Me

You werc there for me when my dad was not,
he wasn't there a lot.

You were there as you can see,
you made me be just plain old me.

You definitely are the coolest Mom,
you stopped me when I was a ticking bomb.

I do not really know what to say,
except I love you, and I hope you stay.

Dedicated to: My mom

Nick Carson

Green Elementary
Goshen, OH
Nominated by fifth grade teacher Mrs. Craigmyle

For Mom, Who's Always There

You are nice,
you always have to tell me more than twice.

You always make me study,
and you'll always be my buddy.

You always tell me to water the dogs,
and Daddy makes me chop logs.

You'll always be there to care for me,
even when I am stuck in a tree.

You always tell me to get a grip,
even after I sneak a sip.

You always rub my tummy,
and it makes me feel less funny.

You'll always tell me what to do,
even after I'm thirty-two.

Most of all, I'll always love you forever,
and hope you and Dad will always be together.

Lindsay Haines

Green Elementary
Goshen, OH
Nominated by fifth grade teacher Jackie Kaldmo

Writer's Block

My head feels like a rock,
I must have writer's block.
I cannot think, I cannot see,
And I cannot even write poetry.
I have no ideas, I have not a clue,
Therefore, I cannot write a poem for you.
Oh, Wait! Wait! Why didn't I see,
This whole time, I've been writing poetry.

Emily Etzkorn

St. Margaret of York
Loveland, OH
Nominated by fifth grade teacher Laura Willis

Sports

Sports, sports, they are great to play,
You can play them any day!
There is golf, tennis, basketball,
Swimming, soccer, and volleyball!
All you need to do is have fun,
You can play them inside, or out in the sun!
You definitely need to play as a team,
Because it really helps your self-esteem!
Sports are great to play with stress,
It relaxes you, unlike games like chess!
So grab some shoes, a shirt, and shorts,
And go outside and play some sports!

Elizabeth Brandel

St. Margaret of York
Loveland, OH
Nominated by fifth grade teacher Jill Murphy

People

People come in all shapes and sizes,
Some for talent, win big prizes.

Some people come from Ecuador,
They could start another war.

People come from all around,
Some of them make a lot of sound.

Some of the people that I know,
Love to go to New Mexico.

Lots of people do CPR,
Some of them are movie stars.

Most people like their beds,
Some of which have bald heads.

People are hard to figure out,
I guess I'm done, it's time to back out.

Sara-Jean Phillips

Morrow Elementary School
Morrow, OH
Nominated by fifth grade teacher Theresa Elliott

Martin Luther King Jr.

M is for minister. That was his occupation.

A is for Atlanta, Georgia.
  He was born and buried there.

R is for rights.
  He worked to change the rights of black people.

T is for theological.
  He went to Crozer Theological Seminary.

I is for "I have a dream."
  He made this speech in 1963.

N is for Nobel Peace Prize. He received it in 1964.

L is for led. Martin Luther King Jr. led many marches.

U is for understanding. He wanted white people to understand his cause.

T is for Henry Thoreau. He wrote a book that Martin based his beliefs on.

H is for honor.
  We have a day in January to honor him.

E is for equality. He believed in equality for all.

R is for James Earl Ray. Ray was accused of killing Martin in 1968.

K is for killed. He was assassinated.
I is for intelligent. He attended college at age fifteen.
N is for nonviolence.
He placed emphasis on "nonviolence."
G is for Gandhi. He took Gandhi's advice.

J is for justice. He lived and died for justice.
R is for reality. He wanted "his dream"
   to become reality.

Roxie Blevins

Morrow Elementary School
Morrow, OH
Nominated by fifth grade teacher Candance Anness

Cats

Cats
are fast
running, clawing, biting
climbing up the trees
Fire trucks

Justin Charles

Williamsburg Elementary
Williamsburg, OH
Nominated by fifth grade teacher Teresa Whiteman

Mothers

Mothers are there to show you they care
and you can count on them to always be there.
They give you all of their heart,
to make sure you have a good start.
I know my mother will always be there to care.

Lydia Barnhart

Williamsburg Elementary
Williamsburg, OH
Nominated by fifth grade teacher Teresa Whiteman

You and Me

I'm writing a poem you see,
It is just about you and me,
About the good old times,
Whcn there were no such thing as rhymes.
When everything was black and white,
Our parents, TV's, puppies and the night.
Now let's go way back when you were General Lee
And I was General Grant,
When we had a tea every fortnight with Sarah,
Your aunt.
Now my frien'
Let us go way back when...when...
Oh dear, I've forgotten!
I think it was a time in which we picked cotton.
Let us go back to today,
Today you must feed the horses hay,
Water the plants,
And sew up my pants!
Now I draw the line at that,
Oh and one more thing, please do feed the cat.
As you can see,
I wrote this poem about you and me!

Elizabeth Culnan

Mercy Montessori Center
Cincinnati, OH
Nominated by fifth grade teacher Carla Booth

Sky Of Life

The stars shine upon the widest sky,
Until the clouds come swiftly by.
Then the rain comes pouring down,
Way down, down to the ground.
It gives the plants the water they need,
So they can live, drink and feed.
Next the clouds go passing by,
And again you can see the starry sky.

Sarah C. Abare

Mercy Montessori Center
Cincinnati, OH
Nominated by fifth grade teacher Carla Booth

The Meaning Of Cats

The meaning of cats,
Is to sit on your lap.
For if they do not,
They will grow fat.
Cats really hate bats,
And they really love rats,
So let your cat
Sit on your lap,
For if you do not,
They will grow fat.
For that is the meaning of cats!

Stephanie Kaminski

Mercy Montessori Center
Cincinnati, OH
Nominated by fifth grade teacher Carla Booth

L ife is like a road with many directions
  for you to follow
I t has its bumps, curves, dead ends and intersections
F or on each road there are many adventures
  or opportunities for you to choose
E ither road you choose, there's always life

Catherine Bauman

Bramble Developmental Academy
Cincinnati, OH
Nominated by fifth grade teacher Rosaland Robinson

Their Journey

Flying high above,
The geese here make their noises.
Now winter is here.

Something's in the air.
Now we know autumn is here.
Leaves and geese on the ground.

Lakes are filled with geese,
Their honking filling the air.
They won't stay for long.

Because spring is here,
Now it's time for their journey.
Home to Canada.

Johanna Michelle Froelicher

Cure' of Ars
Cincinnati, OH
Nominated by fifth grade teacher Fred G. Costa

Winter Birds

The wind is blowing,
And it is almost snowing.
Winter is coming.

The birds will take flight,
Fall is coming to an end.
The birds have flown south.

Some birds like it hot.
The birds stay north or fly south.
Some birds like it cold.

After winter ends,
The earth turns and it gets hot.
All the birds are back.

Shawn Gerard Bosse

Cure' of Ars
Cincinnati, OH
Nominated by fifth grade teacher Fred G. Costa

Ice-Skating

I ce
C old
E legant

S ilver medal
K atarina Witt
A chieve
T ara Lipinski
I ce rink
N agano
G old medal

Elizabeth LaGory

Cure' of Ars
Cincinnati, OH
Nominated by fifth grade teacher Fred G. Costa

The Big Storm

There was a storm tonight,
with lightning all around,
it gave me quite a fright,
as tree limbs hit the ground!

The thunder began to rumble,
and the sky grew very dark,
the wind caused leaves to tremble,
as I walked quickly through the park.

Now the storm has ended,
as we see the morning sun,
the damage must be mended,
so we can once again have fun.

Jacob Brown

St. Dominic School
Cincinnati, OH
Nominated by fifth grade teacher Tamara Fangman

I feel lost and all alone,
very ashamed and out of tone.
No one to talk to, nothing to do.
I am lost, and I need you.
My troubles have doubled,
I am in a lot of pain,
I need you, dear friend,
not someone who is mean and vain.

You always seem to listen,
you never interrupt and glisten
when I say I love you, dear friend,
never go away.

When I went to hug you,
and went to draw you nearer,
I found out that my dear friend
was only just a mirror.

Hollie Wessel

St. John the Evangelist
Cincinnati, OH
Nominated by fifth grade teacher Rosemary Jansen

Fall
beautiful, cold
raking, jumping, falling
colorful leaves on trees
Autumn

Allison Gates

St. Teresa of Avila
Cincinnati, OH
Nominated by fifth grade teacher Carole Eagan

Our Vacation

Mother, Mother for our vacation,
Why don't we visit every nation?
How about China, India, Kalamazoo,
Russia, Japan, and Australia too!

I think Greenland would be very nice.
Or maybe Antarctica, which is made of ice.
Or how about.....
"No!" Mother yelled loudly.
"We're staying here!" she said proudly!

Jenny Frank

St. Teresa of Avila
Cincinnati, OH
Nominated by fifth grade teacher Carole Eagan

One Fun Day

As I play outside with my friends,
I wish the day would never end,
looking up at the clear blue sky,
I noticed the beautiful birds flying high.

We laugh and giggle as we run around,
on the beautiful grass that fills the ground,
the squirrels are running, and playing tag too,
"It's fun to watch them," said my nice friend, Sue.

The day is almost coming to an end,
it's time to say good-bye to my cool friend,
the moon is shining bright I must say,
it has been a long, but very good day.

Ashley Boyce

St. Dominic School
Cincinnati, OH
Nominated by fifth grade teacher Tamara Fangman

The Storm

Here comes a big storm,
but we do not know,
tell us wise weatherman,
will it rain or snow?

The sky may look okay
for about an hour,
but then it might get scary,
and even knock out the power!

The lightning might strike;
the thunder might rumble;
the winds might be strong;
the tornadoes might crumble!

Anthony Stertz

St. Dominic School
Cincinnati, OH
Nominated by fifth grade teacher Tamara Fangman

The Sun

A big ball glowing gold
Warms the earth from winter's cold.
Children began wearing shorts.
Playing many summer sports.
Fishing, swimming, sports.
But don't get burnt by the sun!
During the warm summer nights
There is plenty of soft white light.
Keeping me awake in bed
The light shining on my head.
Then my parents take a peep
And find me sound asleep.

Benjamin Love

Bethany School
Cincinnati, OH
Nominated by fifth grade teacher Sue Kaneaster

The Garden

The garden smells sweet.
Last year we grew a beet.
My brother used it to tickle my feet.
The garden is musical.
It has a good beat.
The hummingbird hums.
It sounds like a couple drums.
The garden bears fruit.
(Some make you toot.)
It all tastes good in my mouth.
Some we grow is from the South.
The garden smells sweet,
and man is it neat!
You can plant it indoors or outdoors,
on any of the three floors.
The garden is nice.
It will die if it is in ice.
But we love our garden, oh so much,
because it supplies us with our lunch.

D. Wells Huskey II

Bethany School
Cincinnati, OH
Nominated by fifth grade teacher Jean Macejko

March Madness Is Driving Me Mad!

March madness is driving me mad!
All these teams I can't hope to remember.
March madness is driving me nuts!
Making predictions and having them ridiculed.
March madness is driving me off the wall!
Seeing my predictions go up in smoke
In a matter of minutes
March madness is driving me batty!
Feeling the bitter sting of defeat
And the sweet warmth of victory
March madness is driving me kooky!
The final four is finally here.
March madness is driving me insane!
The pressure of the championship game is here.
March madness is finally over.
I can't wait until next year!

Sam Westmoreland

Bethany School
Cincinnati, OH
Nominated by fifth grade teacher Jean Macejko

Almond Joy

I have a hamster that is very cute.
He likes to eat all sorts of fruit.
We like to call him Almond Joy.
A paper tube is his favorite toy.
He's really nice,
to be precise.
Sometimes I think that he's a fish,
when I find him swimming in his water dish.

Brittany McGraw

Miami East Intermediate
Casstown, OH
Nominated by fifth grade teacher Gary Weaver

To: Boomer

I know you're my hamster,
I'll give this to you,
for all the nice things
that you can do.

For breaking your wheel,
for running away,
for hiding in the kitchen,
and getting tooth decay.

For eating my chips,
and biting on your cage,
and eating stuff,
like my homework page.

I know you're a hamster,
and you cannot read,
but try to understand,
you're the hamster I need.

Natalie Marie Mogle

Miami East Intermediate
Casstown, OH
Nominated by fifth grade teacher Kim Rupert

Silver

Silver is a tear that falls from a baby's rosy
Cheek that is born at the silver dawn.
It is a button that comes unsewn from a jacket
Passed down from your grandmother, with silver
Replacing her auburn hair.
It is the moon in a starless night
Shining its beams on the round face
Of an innocent sleeping child.
Silver is an angel that whispers to an old man in
A deserted alley, "Come with me."

Lydia Taulbee

Mark Twain Elementary
Miamisburg, OH
Nominated by fifth grade teacher Susan O'Malley

A Win For Lightning (My Special Horse)

We thunder down the track,
There's a horse coming near, but we don't look back.
The homestretch looks so long,
But everything will go our way
And nothing will go wrong.
We're beginning to soar,
As we win, I hear the crowd's roar.
As I ride into the winner's circle, I feel truly worthy,
As the P.A. blasts loudly that Lightning has won
The Kentucky Derby.

Sara Anne Brooks

Mark Twain Elementary
Miamisburg, OH
Nominated by fifth grade teacher Monique Novotny

Wishing From Ellis Island

I wish I had a family,
I wish I had a home.
I wish they'd let me go through,
I wish I won't go home.
I wish the persecution would stop,
I wish it all would end.
I wish I'd pass the examinations,
I wish that I would win.

Amanda Howard

Westlake Elementary School
New Carlisle, OH
Nominated by fifth grade teacher Kimberly Rudd

The Happenings Inside This Helmet

Inside this helmet are touchdowns to be scored.
Injuries waiting to happen.
Fumbles to be recovered.
All-Stars about to shine.
Interceptions, yet to be caught.
Millionaires anticipating payday.
Beads of sweat caused by determination.

Jordan Woosley

Van Cleve Troy
Troy, OH
Nominated by fifth grade teacher Jan Miller

Happiness

Happiness is...
Blue likc summer sky.
Warm like a bubble bath.
Sounds like chirping birds in spring.
Smells like lilacs blooming.
Tastes like garden fresh salad.
Looks like a field of flowers.
Feels like nothing can go wrong.

Katie O'Ryan

Van Cleve Troy
Troy, OH
Nominated by fifth grade teacher Jan Miller

Daily Excuses

I'm loaded down with homework, a ton.
By tryouts tonight, I'll never be done.
Math, geography, and studies galore!
In the morning, I'll have even more.
I have had homework, all through the week.
I could have done it Monday, but I wanted to freak!
Tuesday was such a blur; I had to get a manicure.
Wednesday would have been fine,
but there was a chick flick on channel nine.
Thursday could have been okay,
but I was swimming all day.
Friday would have been great, but I had a date.
So now it's Monday again,
and I'm still not ready to begin.

Lauren Brown

LaMendola Elementary School
Huber Heights, OH
Nominated by fifth grade teacher Darrel Gray

My Life Is Over As I Know It

I'm sick in bed just lying here
An aspirin would do me good,

My doctor says stay off my feet
And eat a lot of food,

I've got to stay in bed today
And boy I don't get paid,

But the worst of all my troubles are
I need a hearing aid.

My skin is wrinkling
My eyes stopped twinkling,

Both my legs are broken
And my swollen feet need soakin',

My gray hair's falling out
And my canes are all about,

My chin is sagging, my smile's in doubt
And all my teeth are falling out,

My wedding ring fell down the drain
And now my wife has gone insane,

My last request is that you pray
For my dear soul that passed away.

Jessica Erin Stumpff

LaMendola Elementary School
Huber Heights, OH
Nominated by fifth grade teacher Darrel Gray

The Ship Of Dreams

There it was,
"The Ship Of Dreams"
the biggest ship you ever seen.

She was big and beautiful,
mighty and strong.
Seven stories high and
a thousand feet long.

They set out to sail
to find their dream,
not knowing what lies
ahead to be.

When disaster struck
in the icy waters,
nothing could save them,
not even a million dollars.

Many had perished
on that frightful night,
while others held on
with all their might.

Many dreams were lost
but may soon be found.
Keeping that dream alive
they are Heaven bound.

The survivors live on
with this I trust,
a new meaning on life
that remains untouched.

And now in closing
this I'll say,
Keep the dream alive, and
Live well, I pray.

Jayce M. Dickens

LaMendola Elementary School
Huber Heights, OH
Nominated by fifth grade teacher Darrel Gray

The Autumn Meadow

As I stand in the autumn meadow,
I feel a cool breeze dancing around me.

I smell a sweet honey smell.
Birds are chirping a soft melody.
The squirrels are gathering acorns for
The long cold winter.

As I look down I see dew on the grass.
It's cold now.
It's windy now.
It's autumn now.

Trishna K. Shah

Dr. John Hole
Centerville, OH
Nominated by fifth grade teacher Maureen Richmond

Flowers

There are pink ones and yellow ones,
All spun with gold.
Gold ones and blue ones,
With treasures untold.
Nothing so beautiful as flowers so bold.

Courtney Tuck

Morrison Elementary
Athens, OH
Nominated by fifth grade teacher Melanie Lunsford

Autumn

Radiating colors red, orange, yellow.
The leaves falling gracefully down
Like a group of parachuters
To the ground.
The smell of winter coming in, and
The dead leaves dying on
The ground make a merry
Crunching sound. As we
Walk we hear their music
Beneath our feet.

Now to the place where
The rabbits hop, a new sight
To see. With the sky open
Above our heads, and a
New burst of yellow
From a tree, the scent
Of rain, the smell of
Dew, and old Jack
Frost creeping too.

On the bare ground
Beneath our feet, the
Goldenrod and violet
Take their last peep before
They bow their head to sleep.

Noah N. Gillespie

Dr. John Hole
Centerville, OH
Nominated by fifth grade teacher Maureen Richmond

Where is my funny bunny?
He got left out in the cold.
Where is my funny bunny?
He's worth a lot of gold.

When my bunny's happy,
He's friendly as can be.
But when my bunny's angry,
You had better flee!

Where's my funny bunny?
He was left out in the rain.
Where's my funny bunny?
He's worth a lot of grain.

When my bunny's gloomy,
He never sleeps at all.
But when my bunny's cheerful
He stays up and has a ball!

Oh, my funny bunny,
Where could he be?
Oh, there's my funny bunny,
Hiding in a tree.

I found my funny bunny!
I'm as happy as can be!
OH NO! I made him angry!
He's gnawing at my knee!

Michael Mazzocca

Morrison Elementary
Athens, OH
Nominated by fifth grade teacher Sheila VanDyke

My People

My people cry out as they're forced to leave their land.
Moms, dads, and children leave their lands.
Oh, what horror!
Paleface men take over.
They live on the Indian's land and take their food
As thousands of Indians die away.

Walking all the way west,
They freeze with cold.
No Indians have warm clothes or food.
Babies cry through the long cold nights.
The paleface living in the nice warm houses.

The trip started in 1830 and carried through to 1840.
They walked and rode horses west.
The walk became known as The Trail of Tears.
About five hundred Cherokees remained,
They didn't know if they could go on to the land
They were going to.
The Cherokees had to start their lives over.
Would you have wanted to be in The Trail of Tears?

Ashley N. Johnson

Amesville Elementary
Amesville, OH
Nominated by fifth grade teacher Patsy Dearing

Horses In The Wild

Horses in the wild like to run free,
But sometimes they have to swim the sea.
Herds can be found galloping away,
Later to be captured and auctioned for pay.
This, they tell me, is done at Chincoteague Bay.
Afterwards, they are brought home, loved,
And fed a great big bale of hay.

Lindsay Hope Garrett

Amesville Elementary
Amesville, OH
Nominated by fifth grade teacher Patsy Dearing

Moonlight

Moonlight is very nice,
When you are sad,
When you are glad.
It does not matter if you are neither,
All you have to be is a believer.
A believer in dreams,
A believer in many things!
You can believe in fairy tales.
Or you could just love the light from the moon.
It does not matter if you don't believe in any of them.
The moonlight holds wishes for everyone,
So keep believing.
One day you will see the dreams
And wishes of everyone,
That loves the moonlight.

Patricia A. Gibson

Amesville Elementary
Amesville, OH
Nominated by fifth grade teacher Patsy Dearing

Snow Day

Beautiful snowflakes
hover over bright houses
while children yell loud.

Shawn Faires Dolan

Homer-Union Elementary School
Glouster, OH
Nominated by fifth grade teacher Jane Armstrong

America

I live in America,
America lives in me.

When America is gone
So will I be.

America is a free land.
It has sand,
It has trees.
There are some bees
Which make honey.

America is the land we love,
The bird of peace is a dove.

If you live in America,
You should be proud,
For America is a good land to be in.

Jenna Correll

St. John Elementary
Delphos, OH
Nominated by fifth grade teacher Susan Yakir

My Brother, Brad

I have a brother named Brad.
He was never bad.
Then one day
He moved away
And everybody was sad.

Brian Metzger

St. John Elementary
Delphos, OH
Nominated by fifth grade teacher Susan Yakir

Rocketing Red

Red is fire and tempers and someone getting burned.
Red is the taste of Popsicles.
Roses and cologne smell red.
Getting embarrassed makes me feel red.
Red is the sound of Dad nagging
and getting yelled at.
Red are hospitals, grill restaurants,
and apple tree farms.
Getting cut is red.
Getting teased is also red.
Red are peppers in your mouth.

William Dean Young

Crestview Elementary
Convoy, OH
Nominated by fifth grade teacher Amy Kinkle

Sam Gribley

Sam Gribley is a twelve-year-old kid
In the woods is where he hid.
He lived in a hemlock tree where
He hoped no one would find him there.
He has a baby falcon that he trained
So it could catch some wild game.

Jessica J. Franks

Wilson Vance Intermediate
Findlay, OH
Nominated by fifth grade teacher Don Schmidt

The Ghost

When the sea felt empty
I wondered why.
He comes to the horizon from a deep, deep dive.
He sends from his blowhole a wonderful sound.
He calls for all others to come around.
He warns them not to go near the big, big boat over there.
He dives down deep then rises too close to the big boat.
For the whalers see him and shoot with their bow.
I feel sorry for the loss that day.
I hope never to hear a story like that
Any day

Bethany Grace Long

Wilson Vance Intermediate
Findlay, OH
Nominated by fifth grade teacher Lori Beth Burnside

The Killer Whale

The killer whale swims through the water
eating fish and dolphins.
It flows without fear.
On his face he starts to grin, and he acts sluggish.
But still, he uses his savage strength
to fight off his enemies,
spluttering and splashing in the
phosphorescent sea.

Michael Bernot

Wilson Vance Intermediate
Findlay, OH
Nominated by fifth grade teacher Lori Beth Burnside

Ma! Don't Throw Those Shoes Out

Ma, don't throw those shoes out!
They're my all-time favorite shoes.
I admit they smell like dog poop,
and mud that's in its grooves.
Half their loops are missing,
and they have a couple of holes.
They could have been attacked
by an angry pack of moles.

Yes! I know that I've outgrown them.
I know they're faded and torn.
I can see the strings are frazzled,
and I'm aware the soles are worn.
These shoes sure mean a lot to me,
and I swear I'll have the blues
if you dare to throw that pair out.
They're my all-time favorite shoes!

Ben Watercutter

Fort Loramie Elementary School
Fort Loramie, OH
Nominated by fifth grade teacher Lori Griesdorn

Feelings

Blue is the feeling of sadness,
Tears trickling down your face on a rainy day,
Depression when a loved one passes away,
They have gone but their soul has stayed,
Blue is like a cold and shivering day.

Debbi Rosengarten

Fort Loramie Elementary School
Fort Loramie, OH
Nominated by fifth grade teacher Lori Griesdorn

If I Were In Charge Of The World

If I were in charge of the world,
I'd cancel politicians, dentists, girls,
And driving at age sixteen.

If I were in charge of the world,
I'd cancel school. I'd cancel junky cars
And foods that taste rotten. I would also cancel
Sleeping with little brothers.

If I were in charge of the world, I'd eat ice cream,
Pizza, and plenty of Mountain Dew.
A person who is good at sports
And likes math would still be allowed to be in charge
Of the world.

Philip Segar

Fort Loramie Elementary School
Fort Loramie, OH
Nominated by fifth grade teacher Lori Griesdorn

Midnight Stalkers

Ruffled tongues and sophisticated minds,
They come in shapes and colors of all kinds.

Wavy tails and sharpened claws,
With slinky bodies and careful paws.

Cats love to explore and make many a find,
And when it comes to lives, cats have nine.

Pointy ears and nimble feet,
Oh, those cats are so neat!

Abby Cupp

Kalida Elementary
Kalida, OH
Nominated by fifth grade teacher Darlene Imm

Basketball

Basketball is quite a rough sport,
A uniform is a T-shirt and shorts.

The ball goes up to start the jump,
If you're not careful you'll end up on your rump.

Ten players it takes to play the game,
A referee, cheerleaders, and fans all the same.

OK, the whistle blows, the game begins,
Back and forth, two points, swish, it's in.

The points are kept up on a scoreboard,
They take the shot, add two more.

We play four quarters back and forth,
The score is close 34 to 34.

One quarter left, I hope we win,
If we don't it would be a sin.

Two more points go up on our score,
That's all we need to win once more.

Greg Recker

Kalida Elementary
Kalida, OH
Nominated by fifth grade teacher Beth Birkemeier

My Horse and Me

In the summer, children play
In the summer, I ride all day.

My horse I groom
The daylight looms.

I dream of the fair, it's coming soon
As I ride my horse beneath the moon.

As I ride my horse out to pasture
It's just her, my friend and I, her master.

The stars are bright on this August night
My horse neighs at the beautiful sight.

I love the summer I feel so free
In the summer it's just my horse and me.

Rachael Amy Paul

New Bremen Elementary School
New Bremen, OH
Nominated by fifth grade teacher Linda Kremer

Spring

Spring is beautiful, spring is nice
I like spring better than anything
Trees turn green and birdies hatch
All the boys go play catch
Flowers pop up in many colors
Then the girls go pick them
For their mothers
Then spring ends
And summer begins
All the children go to the pool
For a swim
And that's all I can say
Because it's no longer spring
It's a summer day.

Sadie Mayer

New Bremen Elementary School
New Bremen, OH
Nominated by fifth grade teacher Linda Kremer

Spring Beginnings

Spring is a special time of year.
The snow starts to disappear.
The temperature begins to warm
And the bees begin to swarm.
The birds begin to sing.
Baseball gets into swing.
Flowers begin to bud.
Rain creates a lot of mud.
The sun begins to shine.
Fishing is real fine.
The grass grows greener.
The bees get meaner.
That's how spring begins.

Kelly Harrod

New Bremen Elementary School
New Bremen, OH
Nominated by fifth grade teacher Linda Kremer

Spring
warm, flowers
biking, gardening, swimming
makes people very happy
Season

Monika Lee Sudman

West Elementary
St. Mary's, OH
Nominated by fifth grade teacher Linda Johnson

Kites Can Fly

Kites can fly! Kites can soar!
From the floor to the sky.
Really, really, really high!
Down and up, and up some more.
It's hard to stop, you know it's true.
Kites are fun for me and you!

Nathan Kitzmiller

West Elementary
St. Mary's, OH
Nominated by fifth grade teacher Susan Nuss

When I Grow Up

When I grow up I want each heart
To be filled with love and laughter...
For each
eye
to have a little child's glow.
For each
ear
to block out the bad and let in
the good.
And for everyone in this world
to love one another,
share with each other
and laugh...... together.

Krista Sanford

West Elementary
St. Mary's, OH
Nominated by fifth grade teacher Nancy Wolfe

A Sneaky Little Crab

There once was a sneaky little crab.
He worked nights in a chemistry lab.
He was purple and red.
One day I found him dead.
So they took him away in a cab.

Maggie Faller

St. Joseph School
Wapakoneta, OH
Nominated by fifth grade teacher Tonya Henderson

Have Pity On That Itty-Bitty Kitty

There once was a very nice kitty.
He was so very itty-bitty.
He loved to ride his bikes.
He got scared and said, "Yikes."
Then he died; it was such a pity.

Hannah Scherger

St. Joseph School
Wapakoneta, OH
Nominated by fifth grade teacher Tonya Henderson

Leaves

Leaves, leaves everywhere,
even in the trees' hair.
Oh...how did they get there?

Katie Toth

St. Joseph School
Wapakoneta, OH
Nominated by fifth grade teacher Tonya Henderson

It

Look! It's It.
See It?
Look at It.
Play with It.
Wash It.
Dry It.
Pet It.
Hug It.
Share It.
Own It.
Draw It.
Feed It.
Talk to It.
Have fun with It.
Throw It.
Catch It.
Pass It.
Push It.
Do anything with It!
Hey, wait a minute.
What is It?

Summer Knapp

East Elementary School
Pendleton, IN
Nominated by fifth grade teachers
Robin Henderson and Teresa Knight

Underwear!

They could be old or sometimes new.
They could be orange or sometimes blue.
They could have Mickey or Donald Duck.
They could be little or sometimes get stuck.
They could be lucky or never be worn.
They could be ratty or sometimes torn.
They could have a dot or a stripe
Or in Daddy's case, be really ripe!
That's my underwear story.
Read it and love it in all its glory.

Jennifer Anson

East Elementary School
Pendleton, IN
Nominated by fifth grade teachers
Robin Henderson and Teresa Knight

African Lion

The lion walks across the plains
Against the Serengeti sunset.
His silhouette is perfectly shaped,
As he stalks his prey.
In daylight he is quiet,
When he raises his great head.
Only once will he roar,
Before lying down to rest.

Alyson Kracke

East Elementary School
Pendleton, IN
Nominated by fifth grade teachers
Robin Henderson and Teresa Knight

A Question Of Love

Some say love isn't true,
But they don't think of my love for you
True or false,
Is the question of love.

Except my love for you,
My love for you is like
A promise never broken,
A tree never dying,
A star never falling.

It never falls or stumbles,
Like a flower it grows,
And like a spirit,
It never dies.

Derek Culbertson

St. Mary
Alexandria, IN
Nominated by fifth grade teacher R. Donald Lynch

Spring

Springtime is a lovely time,
Spring comes alive,
While winter withers and dies.

Leaves are wrestling,
While the wind is bustling,
Kids are playing,
While the trumpets are swaying.

I love springtime,
Laughter in the air,
The sun is shining everywhere.

I love springtime,
It gives you such a glow.
I'd appreciate it more but,
I have too many places to go.

Marisa Harmon

St. Mary
Alexandria, IN
Nominated by fifth grade teacher R. Donald Lynch

Corky's Porky

There once was a man named Corky,
Who loved to eat lots of porky,
He raised some pigs,
And grew some figs,
To eat with his strong, steel forky.

Sarah Marie Noel

Indiana Christian Academy
Anderson, IN
Nominated by fifth grade teacher Jeanne Luttrull

The moon hasn't shone all this night,
So my family started to fight,
I hurt someone's nose,
And ripped my mom's hose,
And that was a horrible sight!!!!

Jami Inholt

Indiana Christian Academy
Anderson, IN
Nominated by fifth grade teacher Jeanne Luttrull

Letters

Letters are fun to write.
They are written day or night.
Letters are said when you're asleep
And even when you're counting sheep.
Letters are part of a story.
They make feelings happy, sad or gory.
They can be with you and your friends.
Letters are something that never ends.
Letters come in all sizes and shapes.
They may be part of something big,
Like gorillas or apes.
Letters are something we always use.
Letters are something we can't refuse.
Letters can be something we do not know.
And letters can help our knowledge to grow.
We use letters to read, write and spell.
Without letters we would dwell
In a world that's not so swell.
Letters are in the soup I just ate.
Letters also help us to communicate.
Letters are something we will always love.
Letters spell the symbol of love -- the turtledove.

Kent Smith

Roosevelt Elementary
McDonald, OH
Nominated by fifth grade teacher Connie Morris

Thankful, thankful for this day,
Thankful, thankful anyway.
Thankful, thankful every year.
Thankful, thankful for being here.
Thankful, thankful for my hair.
Thankful, thankful for what I have to wear.

Korey Raimey

Roosevelt Elementary
Warren, OH
Nominated by fifth grade teacher Bobbie Patterson

Today We Go To Church

We go to church to sing and pray,
We will go to church today.
It is held on each Sunday,
We will go to church today.
We take that time to praise our God,
We will go to church today.
Bells ringing, choirs singing,
We will go to church today.
Hurry children, don't delay,
For we will go to church today.

Lura E. Abbott

St. Margaret of York
Loveland, OH
Nominated by fifth grade teacher Laura Willis

Praying Mantis

Praying mantis, praying mantis, how do you do?
I think it's neat just looking at you.
You're up there so high on our barn door,
Please don't fall down and hit the floor.

I'm so amazed watching you climb up my arm,
Because I know that you will do me no harm.
I wonder why there's only one of you,
And, why don't you come in groups of two?

I like it better when I am with a friend,
Maybe you have one around the bend?
I like it when I put you down,
I can watch you fly all around.

I like your overcoat of pale green,
No, it doesn't make you look mean.
Watch out for that baseball, here it comes,
If Dad doesn't catch it, you're all done!

Brittany Ream

Marshallville Elementary
Marshallville, OH
Nominated by fifth grade teacher Thomas Cleary